Contents

Introduction

Dantes stood up and looked in front of the boat. Three hundred feet away, he saw the black and frightening shape of the rock where the Chateau d'If stands. The prison was about 300 years old. 'People tell many strange stories about this place,' Dantes thought. 'Prisoners go there and never return. Is this the end of all hope?'

Edmond Dantes is a young seaman. His enemies tell the government that he wants to help Napoleon return to France as its ruler. So, on the day of his wedding to the beautiful Mercedes, Edmond is thrown into the prison at the Chateau d'If. There he meets a man who tells him about some treasure on the island of Monte Cristo. Will Edmond escape from the prison and find the treasure? And will he return to his home and family in Marseilles?

This exciting adventure story takes place in France in the 1800s. In 1814 France's ruler, Napoleon, was sent by his enemies to the island of Elba. Those enemies – Prussia, Russia, Britain, Austria, Sweden and other countries – brought Bourbon kings back to France. But most French people did not like these new rulers, and Napoleon knew this. In 1815, the year when this story begins, he decided to return to France.

Napoleon landed in Cannes. His friends joined him there, and he went to Paris. The king, Louis XVIII, left the country. Napoleon reached Paris on 20th March, and became the ruler of France for a hundred days. When he lost a great fight at Waterloo, his enemies sent him to the island of St Helena.

There is another real person in this book, Cesare Borgia. The Borgia family played an important part in Italian history. Cesare Borgia was born in 1475. His father, Rodrigo Borgia, became Pope Alexander VI in 1492. Cesare was a politician and a soldier.

He fought for and won a number of Italian cities, but he was a hard, unkind ruler. After his father died, Cesare went to prison. Later, he escaped to Spain and fought for the King of Navarre.

The prison of the Chateau d'If stands at the entrance to the old port of Marseilles. This was, in the past, a prison for 'important prisoners, enemies of the king', as Edmond Dantes says. Today it holds no prisoners, but many readers of *The Count of Monte Cristo* visit the place.

The writer of this book was one of two famous French writers called Alexandre Dumas. They were father and son. Dumas *père* (the father) wrote *The Count of Monte Cristo* and many other stories.

He was born in 1802. His father was a soldier with Napoleon, but he died in 1806 and left very little money for his family. Dumas *père* went to school for a short time, but at the age of sixteen he started work. He worked for the Duke of Orleans. He read a lot of books, and he liked Shakespeare's plays and the stories of Sir Walter Scott very much.

Dumas enjoyed travel and adventure. He joined Garibaldi in Sicily in 1860. He was part of Garibaldi's fight to make Italy into 'one great country'. This was the same 'great country' that Faria dreams of in *The Count of Monte Cristo*. Dumas died in France in 1870.

Dumas is most famous for his plays and for his stories about historical people and places. *The Three Musketeers* (1844) was, for example, the first of a number of books about France in the 1600s. His stories are full of adventure and excitement, and there are films and radio and television plays of many of his books.

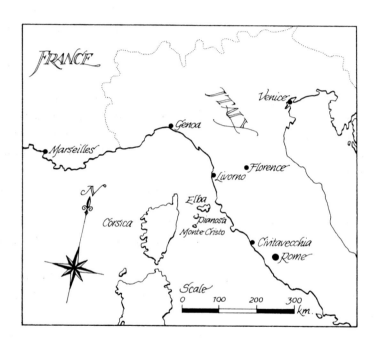

Chapter 1   The Ship Comes Home

On 24th February 1815 the ship *Pharaoh* came in to Marseilles. A man on the shore jumped into a boat and went out to the ship.

A young man, about twenty years old, looked over the side of the ship. He seemed to be the captain. He was the type of man who meets danger without fear.

'Oh! Is it you, Dantes?' cried the man in the boat. 'What has happened?'

'A very sad thing, Mr Morrel,' replied the young man. 'When our ship was near Civitavecchia, we lost our brave Captain Leclerc.'

He turned to his men and gave a quick order. Then he turned again to Morrel. The *Pharaoh* was Morrel's ship, and Edmond Dantes was First Officer.

'We will all die one day, Edmond,' said Morrel. 'The goods–?'

'They are safe, Mr Morrel. Now, come on board. Here is Danglars. He does all the buying and selling. I must look after my ship.'

Morrel climbed quickly onto the ship and met Danglars. Danglars was about twenty-five years old. Nobody on the *Pharaoh* liked him.

'Well, Mr Morrel,' said Danglars. 'You heard about the sad death of Captain Leclerc?'

'Yes. He was a brave and good man.'

'And a good seaman. He was old and wise, a good ship's captain for Morrel and Son,' replied Danglars.

'A young man can be a good captain, too,' Morrel said. 'Look at our friend Edmond. He works well.'

'Yes,' said Danglars. He looked at Dantes. He did not like him. 'Yes, he is young and he is very sure of himself. When the captain died, we had to take orders from him. And as a result, we lost a day and a half at the island of Elba. We needed to come straight to Marseilles.'

'He has to take the captain's place,' said Morrel. 'He is the First Officer. But it was wrong to stop at Elba. Was the ship unsafe? Did you need to work on it?'

'There was nothing wrong with the ship. We stopped at Elba and went on shore. It was a holiday, not work!'

'Dantes,' the shipowner called. 'Come here, please.'

'In a minute, Mr Morrel,' answered Dantes. He gave an order to his men. When the ship was safely tied up, Dantes came towards Morrel. 'The ship is now ready,' he said. 'Can I help you, sir?'

Danglars took a few steps back. 'Why did you stop at the island of Elba?' asked Morrel.

'I don't know, Mr Morrel. It was Captain Leclerc's last order. He gave me a letter for Marshal Bertrand.'

Morrel took Dantes' arm and pulled him close. 'And how is Napoleon?' he said quietly.

'He seemed very well.'

'You spoke to him?'

'No, he spoke to me,' said Dantes. 'He asked: "When did you leave Marseilles? What goods are on board?" He was very interested. Perhaps he wanted to buy the ship. "I am only the First Officer," I said. "The ship belongs to Morrel and Son." "Ah!" he said, "I know them. The Morrels have owned ships for many years. But there was a Morrel who was a soldier. He fought with me at Valence." '

'True!' cried Morrel, happily. 'That was Policar Morrel, my uncle. He was a great soldier, a captain. Dantes, my uncle will be very happy about Napoleon. It will bring fire into the old soldier's eyes. You were right to stop at Elba, Dantes. But don't tell people about the letter for Marshal Bertrand, and about Napoleon. You will get into trouble.'

'Why?' asked Dantes. 'I don't know what was in the letter. Napoleon only asked me simple questions. Anyone can answer questions like those.'

'My dear Dantes,' said the owner, 'are you now free?'

'Yes, Mr Morrel,' Dantes replied.

'Can you come and have dinner with me?'

'Thank you, Mr Morrel. But I must visit my father first.'

'Visit your father, and then come to my house.'

'Thank you again, Mr Morrel. But there is another person that I must see.'

'True, Dantes. I forgot. Of course − the beautiful Mercedes. She came to see me three times. She wanted news about the *Pharaoh*.'

'She has promised to marry me,' the young seaman said.

'My dear Edmond,' said the owner, 'that is very good news. Now hurry away to see your father.'

'Thank you, Mr Morrel. I have a question. Can I leave the ship for fourteen days?'

'To get married?' Morrel asked.

'Yes, first. And then I want to go to Paris.'

'Yes, of course, Dantes. But come back again in one month. The *Pharaoh* can't sail without her captain.'

'Without her captain!' cried Dantes. His eyes were bright and he was very happy. 'Are you really going to make me captain of the *Pharaoh*? Oh, Mr Morrel! I thank you for my father and for Mercedes.'

'Good, Edmond. Go to your father, go and see Mercedes, and then come to see me.'

'Shall I take you to the shore with me?' Dantes asked.

'No, thank you. I'll stay and do some work with Danglars. Were you pleased with him on this journey?'

'Do you mean, "Is Danglars a good friend?" No, we aren't friends. We disagreed one day near the island of Monte Cristo, and he doesn't like me. But he works well. I can say nothing against him.'

The shipowner watched Dantes until he reached the shore. Danglars stood on the ship behind Morrel. He also watched the young man as he went away. But he did not look kindly at Dantes.

Chapter 2   Father and Son

Dantes turned into a narrow street and went into a small house.

'My dear Edmond,' cried his father. 'My boy, my son! You are here in Marseilles! Tell me all your news.'

'I have some sad news. The good Captain Leclerc is dead. But I am now captain of the *Pharaoh*! Just think! I am only twenty years old and the captain of a great ship. I will earn good money. I can buy you a new house. What is the matter, father? Aren't you well?'

'It is nothing,' his father said.

'You need food and a drink. Where will I find food and drink for you?'

'There is nothing in the house,' answered the old man. 'But I don't need anything, because you are here.'

'When I left, three months ago, I gave you plenty of money,' Dantes said.

'Yes. But I paid some money back to our friend Caderousse. He asked me for it.'

'But you gave Caderousse more than half of the money! Why did you do that? Here, father, take this and send for some food.' Edmond put all his money on the table.

'No, no,' said the old man. 'I don't need all that money. But here comes Caderousse. He knows that you are home. He wants to welcome you.'

'Hello! You have returned, Edmond?' Caderousse said.

'Yes, neighbour,' replied Dantes. He tried to hide his real feelings. 'I am ready to help you in any way.'

'You are rich now,' said Caderousse, looking hungrily at the money on the table.

'Oh that,' said Dantes. 'That is my father's money. But of course, you are our neighbour. If you want money, we will lend it to you.'

'Thank you, but I don't need anything. I met my friend Danglars. So I heard that you were here. I wanted to see you.'

'Good Caderousse!' said the old man. 'He is a great friend to us.'

There was an ugly look on Caderousse's face. 'Well, Morrel is pleased with you,' he said. 'Are you hoping to be the next captain of the *Pharaoh*?'

'Yes. I believe that I will be the next captain. But, dear father, I must leave you. Now I must visit another person in the town.'

'Go, my dear boy. And God protect your wife.'

'His wife!' said Caderousse. 'She isn't his wife yet. Mercedes is a fine girl, and fine girls have plenty of young men. But, you will be captain of the *Pharaoh*, so—'

'My opinion of women – and of Mercedes – is better than yours,' Dantes said. 'I know that she will always love me.'

Edmond left the house, and Caderousse joined Danglars. The seaman was waiting for him at the corner.

'He isn't captain yet,' said Danglars quietly. 'We can stop him. Let's go. We will stop at "La Resérve" and drink a glass of wine there.'

'Right, then,' Caderousse said. 'But *you* must pay for the drink.'

Chapter 3   Mercedes

Danglars and Caderousse sat at a table under a tree. In a house about a hundred metres away, a young girl was at the window. Her hair was as black as night, and her eyes were as dark and wonderful as the shadow of a forest.

'Mercedes!' a voice shouted happily outside the house. 'Mercedes!'

'Ah!' cried the girl. And she ran to the door and opened it. 'Here, Edmond, here I am!'

Edmond took Mercedes in his arms. The golden sunshine of Marseilles shone on them. They were together, the only two people in the world.

Edmond and Mercedes walked past 'La Resérve'. Caderousse and Danglars were still there.

'Hey, Edmond!' cried Caderousse. He got up from his seat. 'Are you too proud to speak to your friends?'

'No, my dear man!' Dantes replied. 'I am not proud, but I am happy. I was thinking about Mercedes.'

'When is the wedding?' asked Danglars.

'Soon – tomorrow or the next day, here at "La Resérve". We hope that you and Caderousse will be there.'

'Tomorrow or the next day! You are in a hurry, captain,' said Danglars.

'I am not a captain yet, Danglars,' said Dantes. 'But, yes, we are in a hurry because I must go to Paris.'

'To Paris! Do you have business there?'

'It is not my business. Captain Leclerc asked me to finish some work for him.'

'Yes, yes, I understand,' said Danglars. And he added, speaking to himself, 'To Paris – he is taking Marshal Bertrand's letter there. Ah! I have an idea. Dantes, my friend, you are not captain of the *Pharaoh* yet!' He turned towards Edmond. 'A good journey!' he cried.

'Thank you, my friend,' said Edmond. And the two lovers continued on their happy path.

'Boy,' shouted Danglars, 'bring me a pen and paper.'

'It is a strange thought,' said Caderousse. 'You can kill a man with a knife, but you can also kill him with that pen!'

'I will tell you what I am going to do,' said Danglars. 'Dantes has just returned from a journey. He stopped at the island of Elba. We are going to send a letter to an officer of the government. We will write that Dantes is working for Napoleon. He wants to bring Napoleon back as ruler of France.'

Danglars wrote, using his left hand:

> *A friend of the king has information for the king's officers. Edmond Dantes, of the ship* Pharaoh, *brought a letter from Elba to the followers of Napoleon in Paris. You will find the letter in his coat, or at his father's house, or in his room on the ship.*

He put the letter in an envelope and wrote a name on it: *Villefort.*

'So, I have done it,' Danglars said.

'Yes, you have done it,' said Caderousse. 'But it is a dirty piece of work.' He put out his hand to take the letter.

◆

The cooks at 'La Resérve' prepared a wonderful meal for the wedding. Many of the men from the *Pharaoh* were there, and other friends of Dantes.

'Shall we start?' asked the sweet silvery voice of Mercedes. 'We must go to the church.'

Everyone in the party stood up and began to form a line.

Suddenly, there was a loud noise. A man knocked on the door and shouted, 'Open this door, in the name of the law!'

7

An officer came in. There were four soldiers with him.

'Where is Edmond Dantes?'

'That is my name,' said Edmond. 'Why?'

'I can't tell you. Someone will tell you the reason later.'

'Don't be afraid, my good friends,' said Dantes. 'They are making a mistake. That is all, I am sure.'

Dantes went into the courtyard with the soldiers.

'God go with you, my dearest,' cried Mercedes.

'And with you, sweet Mercedes. We shall soon meet again.'

Chapter 4   The Judge

Villefort, the judge, took a paper from one of the men. He said, 'Bring in the prisoner.'

Dantes came into the room. 'Who and what are you?' Villefort asked.

'My name is Edmond Dantes,' the young man replied. 'I am an officer of the *Pharaoh*, one of Morrel's ships.'

'Your age?'

'Twenty.'

'Where were you when the soldiers came?'

'I was at my wedding.' Dantes' voice was full of tears. Earlier in the day he was so happy and now ...

'It is sad that this man missed his wedding,' thought Villefort. But he continued: 'Do you work for Napoleon?'

'I wanted to join one of his ships, but he lost power.'

'People think that you are a dangerous man. They say you want to bring Napoleon back to power.'

'Me? Dangerous! I am only twenty. I don't know about things like power. I love my father, I love Morrel, and most of all I love Mercedes. That is all that I can tell you.'

'Have you any enemies?'

'Enemies?' said Dantes. 'Only important men have enemies. I am not important.'

'True, you are only twenty,' Villefort said. 'But you will soon be captain of a ship. You are marrying a pretty girl. Does someone hate you because you are so lucky?'

'Perhaps. I don't know. You know men better than I do.'

'I received this letter. Do you know the writing?'

Dantes read it. A cloud of sadness passed over his face.

'No, I don't know the writing. But the writer of this letter is a real enemy.'

'Now,' said the judge, 'answer me. Are the words in this letter true?'

'No,' Dantes replied. 'I will tell you the facts. Captain Leclerc became ill soon after we left Naples. On the third day he was very ill. He called me and said, "Promise me something. It is very important." I promised. "After my death, you will become captain. Go to Elba and ask for Marshal Bertrand. Give him this letter, and he will give you another letter. He will tell you where to take it." That is what Captain Leclerc said.'

'And what did you do then?' the judge asked.

'I agreed. Leclerc was dying. On a ship, the last request of an officer is an order. I reached Elba and I went on shore alone. I gave the letter to Marshal Bertrand. He gave me a letter to take to a person in Paris. I came here, visited Mercedes and prepared for my wedding. I am going to Paris tomorrow.'

'Ah,' said Villefort. 'Perhaps you were unwise, but you followed the last orders of your captain. Give me the letter that you brought from Elba. Promise to see me again if I call you. You can go back to your friends now.'

'I am free, then?' said Dantes happily.

'Yes, but first give me the letter.'

'You have it already. The soldiers took it with some other letters. They are on the table.'

'Stop,' said Villefort, as Dantes took his hat. 'Whose name and address are on the letter?'

'Noirtier, Heron Road, Paris.'

Villefort's face went white, and he looked afraid. 'Noirtier!' he said in a weak voice. 'Noirtier!'

'Yes. Do you know him?'

'No,' replied Villefort. 'I am a true follower of the king. I don't know men who want to destroy him.'

'Noirtier wants to destroy the king?' Dantes began to feel afraid. 'I told you – I didn't read the letter. I don't know what it says.'

'Yes, but you saw the name on the envelope.'

'Of course, I read the name. I had to give it to Noirtier.'

'Did you show this letter to anyone?' asked Villefort.

'No. I didn't show it to anyone. I promise you.' Dantes looked at Villefort's face and was afraid.

Villefort read the letter, then he covered his face with his hands. 'Oh!' the judge thought. 'Does he know what is in this letter? Does he know my real name? Does he know that Noirtier is my father? If he knows this, then I am in danger!' He looked closely at Dantes. Then he said, 'You cannot leave now. You must stay here for some time. I will try to make your stay as short as possible. The only thing against you is this letter.' He took the letter from the table, and went to the fire. 'Look, I am burning it.'

'Oh,' cried Dantes, 'you are very kind.'

'Listen,' said Villefort. 'You know that I will help you. You will stay here until this evening. Don't answer any questions, don't say a word about this letter, and don't say the name of Noirtier.'

'I promise.'

Villefort called out, and a soldier came into the room.

'Follow this soldier,' Villefort told Dantes.

The door closed and Villefort fell into a chair. 'Oh, my father.

If people hear about this letter, it will be the end for me. I must make sure that nobody knows about it!'

Chapter 5   The Prison

The soldier took Dantes to a small room. Then, at about ten o'clock, an officer and four soldiers took him through the streets to the shore. They put Dantes in a boat. Then they watched him as the boat moved away.

'What is happening?' Edmond thought wildly. 'The judge was kind to me. He told me not to be afraid. He only told me not to say the name Noirtier. And he destroyed the letter in front of me.'

Dantes looked into the darkness. They were going out to sea. They were sailing away from everything that he loved. He turned to the nearest soldier.

'Friend,' he said, 'please tell me where we are going. I am Edmond Dantes, a seaman, and a man who loves God and the king. Tell me where we are going.'

'You were born in Marseilles and you are a seaman. But you don't know where you are going? Look!'

Dantes stood up and looked in front of the boat. A hundred metres away, he saw the black and frightening shape of the rock where the Chateau d'If stands. The prison was about 300 years old. 'People tell many strange stories about this place,' Dantes thought. 'Prisoners go there and never return. Is this the end of all hope?'

'I am not going to be a prisoner there!' cried Dantes. 'Only important prisoners, enemies of the king, go there! Mr Villefort promised me—'

'Mr Villefort told us to take you to the Chateau d'If.'

The boat reached the shore. A soldier jumped out, took

Dantes' arms and pushed him up some steps. He passed through a door and the door closed behind him.

He was in a courtyard with high walls on all sides. He heard the feet of soldiers, walking around outside.

'Where is the prisoner?' a voice said. 'Follow me.'

Dantes followed. The man took him to a room which was almost under the ground.

'This is your room for tonight,' the man said. 'It is late, and the governor is asleep. Tomorrow, perhaps, he will send you to another place. There is bread and water and some dry grass to sleep on. Good night.'

The man left quickly and took away his lamp. Dantes was alone in the darkness and the silence.

◆

At the first light of day, the guard returned. Dantes was standing in the same place, just inside the door. The man touched Dantes on the arm and asked, 'Haven't you slept?'

'I don't know,' Dantes answered.

The guard looked at him. 'Are you hungry?'

'I don't know.'

'Do you want anything?'

'I want to see the governor.'

The guard gave a short laugh, and left the room. The door closed. Dantes threw himself on the floor. 'What is happening?' he cried. 'Why am I in this place?'

The day passed. Dantes did not eat. He walked round and round the small room.

The next morning, the guard came back again. 'Prisoner,' he said, 'are you feeling better today?'

Dantes did not answer.

'Be brave, man. Can I get you anything?' the guard asked.

'I want to see the governor.'

'That is not possible,' the guard said.

'What can I do, then?' Dantes asked.

'You can have better food – if you pay for it – and books. And you can walk around in the courtyard.'

'I don't want books. This food is all right. And I don't want to walk around. I want to see the governor.'

'You can't. Don't ask to see him. I will always say no. You will go crazy.'

'You think so?'

'I know it. There is a man in this prison – he was in this room before you. "If you help me, I will give you a lot of treasure," he told the governor. He was put in a room underground two years ago.'

'Listen. I am not crazy,' Dantes said. 'And I must see the governor.'

'Oh, ho!' cried the guard, stepping back. 'You *are* going crazy. We will have trouble with you. But there are plenty of places underground.'

He went out. A few minutes later, he returned with four soldiers.

'The governor has sent orders,' he said. He turned to the soldiers. 'This prisoner is crazy. Put him underground.'

The soldiers took Dantes' arms. He went quietly. They walked down fifteen steps. Then the soldiers opened the door of a room, and threw Dantes inside.

The door closed, and Dantes walked around. He held his hands out until he touched the wall. Then he sat down in a corner. It was very dark and he could see nothing

'The guard is right,' he thought. 'This place will make me completely crazy.'

Chapter 6   Underground

Time passed. The chief officer of prisons visited the prisoners' rooms. 'Is the food good?' he asked the prisoners. 'Do you want anything?'

'The food is very bad, and we want to be free,' they all replied.

The officer laughed and turned to the governor. 'Why do we come here? We always hear the same thing. "The food is bad. I have done nothing wrong. I want to be free." Are there any other prisoners?'

'Yes, there are the crazy prisoners. We keep them underground. They are a danger to other people.'

'Let's visit them. I must see them all.'

Two soldiers took the officer down the steps. The air smelled bad. The darkness was full of the smell of death.

'Oh!' cried the officer. 'Who can live here?'

'Very bad men. We must watch them very carefully.'

This was the officer's first visit.

'Prisoner number 34. Let's visit this one first,' he said.

Dantes was sitting in the corner of his room. He looked up and saw the stranger with two soldiers.

'This is an important officer,' he thought. He jumped up to meet him, but the soldiers pushed him back.

'The officer thinks that I am crazy,' Dantes thought. He looked at the officer. He tried to make his voice quiet and calm. 'I only want to know what is going to happen to me. Why am I here? Give me your permission to see a judge.'

'Perhaps,' said the chief officer. Then, turning to the governor, he said, 'Show me your books. What is this man's crime?'

'I know that you can't free me,' said Dantes. 'But tell me, please, that there is hope.'

'I can't tell you that. I can only promise to ask about the matter. Who gave orders for you to come to the prison?'

'Mr Villefort.'

'Does he have a reason to be your enemy?'

'No. He was very kind to me,' Dantes said.

'Then I can believe what he writes about you in the prison's book?'

'Yes.'

The officer left the room and closed the door. But he left something in the room – hope.

The officer kept his promise to Dantes. He looked in the prison book and found:

> EDMOND DANTES: *A dangerous man. He helped Napoleon return from Elba. Watch him carefully.*

'I can't help this prisoner,' the chief officer thought. He wrote in the book:

> *Do nothing.*

Chapter 7   Number 27

Days and weeks passed. Dantes began to think that the officer's visit was only a dream.

Suddenly, one evening, at about nine o'clock, Edmond heard a sound in the wall next to his bed. He listened. 'Perhaps this is only a dream, too,' he thought. But he heard the sound again. He heard something fall – and then silence.

Some hours later, he heard the noise again, nearer and more clearly. Edmond listened. 'I know what that sound is,' he thought. 'A prisoner is trying to escape.'

Edmond wanted to help. He moved his bed, then he looked round the room for a sharp tool. The only things in the room were a bed, a chair, a table, and a water pot. 'I will break the water pot and use one of the sharp pieces,' he thought.

He threw the pot on the floor, and it broke into pieces. He hid two or three pointed bits in his bed.

The next morning, the guard came into the room.

'The water pot fell from my hands when I was drinking,' Dantes said. The man was angry with him for his carelessness, but he brought another pot. He did not take away the broken pieces of the old one.

Dantes started to work. The stone wall was old and soft, and it broke into small pieces easily. At last he pulled a stone out of the wall. It left a hole half a metre wide. He carefully carried all the small pieces of stone into the corners of the room, and covered them with earth. He put back the big stone, and placed his bed in front of the hole.

Later, the guard came with his evening meal. When the man left the room, Dantes started to work again. He worked all night, making a deep hole in the wall. Then he stopped.

'What is this?' he cried. 'I can't cut through it or move it.'

It was a great piece of wood. Dantes could not make the hole deeper.

'Oh, my God, my God!' he cried. 'I want to die. I have lost all hope.'

'Who is the man who can talk at the same time about God and about hopelessness?' said a voice under the earth.

Edmond got up on his knees. 'Ah!' he said. 'A voice – the voice of a man! In the name of God, speak again!'

'Who are you?' said the voice.

'An unhappy prisoner.'

'Why are you in prison?'

'I did nothing wrong,' Dantes replied. 'They say that I tried to help Napoleon. He wanted to return to France.'

'To return to France! Where is he now, then?'

'They sent him to the island of Elba in 1814. Don't you know that? When did you come here?'

'In 1811.'

'Four years before me!'

'Don't do any more work,' said the voice. 'Just tell me – how high up are you?'

'At the same height as the floor of my room,' Dantes said.

'What is behind the door of your room?'

'A narrow room and then the courtyard.'

'Oh! That is bad,' the voice said. 'My plan is wrong. I wanted to break through to the outside wall of the prison.'

'And then?'

'And then throw myself into the sea and swim to one of the islands near here. Cover the opening of the hole in the wall. Do it carefully. Stop working on the hole. Wait until you hear from me again.'

'Tell me who you are,' cried Edmond.

'I am – I am Number 27.'

'Why don't you tell me your name?'

Edmond heard a quiet laugh. 'Oh!' he cried. 'Please – please don't leave me alone. I promise that I won't say a word to the guards.'

'I will talk to you again,' said the voice. 'Tomorrow.'

Edmond closed the opening in the wall, carefully hid the bits of stone and put his bed back in its place.

The next morning, when he moved his bed away from the wall, he heard a sound. He got down on his knees.

'Is it you?' he said. 'I am here.'

Soon after that, part of the floor of Dantes' room fell away. Stones and earth fell down into the opening. Then, at the bottom of the hole, Dantes saw the arms and head of a man. The man climbed up into the room.

Dantes reached his hands out to his new friend. He was a

small man, and his hair was white. His eyes were dark, and he had a long beard. He was not strong.

'You seem very happy to see me!' he said to Dantes. 'Your happiness touches my heart.'

But Dantes knew that the man was very sad. 'You worked hard to escape,' he said, 'but you haven't reached the outside of the prison. This is just another room. But there are three other sides to the room. Do you know what is outside those walls?'

'One wall is built against the rock. One is against the lower part of the governor's house. If we get out there, the guards will catch us. And this side faces – where?'

They looked at the third side of the room. There was a small window high up in the wall, with three strong bars across it.

The man pulled the table across the room and put it under the window. 'Climb on the table,' he said to Dantes. 'Put your back against the wall, and join your hands in front of your body.'

Then prisoner Number 27 jumped up on to the table, and from there on to Dantes' hands and from them onto Dantes' shoulders. He put his head through the top bars of the window, then pulled his head back quickly. Finally he said, 'I thought so.' He got down quickly and easily.

'He moves as quickly as a young man,' Dantes thought.

'This side of your room,' said Number 27, 'faces an open pathway. A soldier guards it day and night. It is not possible to escape through any of these walls.'

Dantes looked at the man. 'You really want to escape,' he thought. 'And now you know that you can't. So why are you so calm?' Then he said, 'Tell me, please – who are you?'

'My name is Faria,' the other man replied. 'I came to the Chateau d'If in the year 1811. Before that, I was in the prison of Fenestrelle for three years.'

'But why are you here?'

'As you know, there are a number of small countries in Italy.

Each country has a ruler. I wanted to make Italy one great country under one great king. My chosen king tried to destroy me. And now Italy will never be one country. Napoleon tried to make it one country, but he did not complete his work. Poor Italy.' The old man's voice was very sad.

'Can I see your secret path behind the wall?' Dantes asked.

'Follow me,' said Faria, and he went into the deep hole in the wall.

Dantes followed.

Chapter 8   Faria's Room

The two friends passed easily along the underground path. Faria pulled up a stone in the floor, and they climbed into his room.

Dantes looked around. 'There is one thing that I still don't understand,' he said. 'How do you do so much work?'

'I work all night.'

'At night? Do you have cat's eyes? Can you see in the dark?'

'No, of course not. But God has given man a mind. With it, we can make what we need. I made a lamp for myself. I get the oil from my food, and it burns very well.'

They sat and talked. Faria's words were clever and wise. Sometimes Dantes could not understand them.

'You are very wise. Will you teach me?' Dantes asked. 'I don't want you to get tired of me. A clever person doesn't want to talk to a person who knows nothing. Teach me, and then the hours will pass more quickly for you.'

Dantes learned new ideas from Faria very quickly and easily. He learned about the history of the world, and the English language, and many other things.

◆

Time passed. Dantes was much happier, but Faria's health was not good. One day, Faria was in Edmond's room. Edmond was working on the secret path between their rooms. Suddenly, Edmond heard Faria cry out in pain. He hurried to him, and found him in the middle of the room. His face was as white as death.

'What is the matter?' cried Dantes.

'Quick!' replied Faria. 'Listen to me.'

Dantes looked at Faria's face and was afraid. Faria's eyes were dark, and there were deep blue circles round them. His skin was very pale.

'Listen,' said Faria. 'I have a terrible illness. I was ill before I came to the prison. Help me back to my room. Take out one of the feet which hold up my bed. There is a small bottle of red liquid in the hole.'

Dantes acted quickly. He pulled the old man down into the underground path, and took him back to his room. Then he helped Faria on to the bed.

'Thank you,' the poor man said. He was very cold now. 'Now I must tell you about this illness. When it reaches its worst point – and not before – I pour a little of the liquid into my mouth.'

He stopped talking. The frightening greyness of death passed over his face. Dantes waited. Then he thought, 'My friend is nearly dead.' He took Faria's knife, broke open the bottle and poured a little of the liquid into Faria's mouth. Then he waited again. 'Will my friend die?' he cried.

One hour passed, and there was no change. Then at last a little colour came into Faria's face. The wide-open eyes showed some life. Faria could not speak, but he pointed to the door. Dantes listened, and heard the steps of the guard. 'He mustn't find me here!' he thought.

The young man ran to the opening of the underground path and hurried to his room. Just after he reached it, the guard came in with food. He saw his prisoner sitting, as usual, on the side of his bed.

After the guard left, Dantes hurried back to Faria's room. He lifted up the stone, and was soon next to the sick man's bed. Faria was a little better, but he was still very weak.

'Don't lose hope,' said Dantes. 'You will soon be strong again.' He sat down on the bed next to Faria and held the old man's cold hands.

'No,' said Faria. 'My first illness lasted for only half an hour. When it ended, I got up from my bed without help. Now I can't move my right arm or leg, and there is a pain in my head. Next time, the illness will kill me.'

Chapter 9   The Story of the Treasure

The next morning, Dantes returned to Faria's room. Faria looked a little better. He showed Dantes a small piece of paper. Half of it was burnt away.

Edmond said, 'I can't see anything except broken lines and words.'

'I know what the words mean,' said Faria. 'But first I will tell you the story of this paper. I was the friend and helper of Prince Spada, the last of the princes of that name. I was very happy with him. A long time ago, his family was very rich – people often say, "as rich as a Spada" – but my friend, Prince Spada, had very little money. He told me about another Spada; this man lived – and died – at the time of Cesare Borgia.

'Cesare Borgia needed money for his wars, but the country was very poor. Finally he thought of a plan. He asked two famous rich men, Rospigliosi and Spada, to dinner. Rospigliosi was very pleased, but Spada was a wise man. "Cesare Borgia wants my money," he thought. "He will kill me." He wrote a note, then he

On May 25th 1498. Ce
invited me to dinner. He
me. He wants all my
When I die give everything to
It is hidden safely on the island
Guido knows the place because
it together. All my gold and
Lift up the twenty-second ro
beach at the east end of
Find the steps that go
Break into the second room
is in the north east corner

Cesare
May

went to the dinner. There was death in the glass of wine in front of him. "If I don't drink the wine, Borgia will kill me in another way," he thought. So Spada drank – and died.

'Cesare Borgia took all the dead man's papers, and the last letter that Spada wrote before the dinner. This said:

I give everything to my brother's child – all my money and all my books. Tell him to keep the prayer book with the gold corners carefully. It will help him to remember his uncle.'

'Cesare looked everywhere. There were some gold cups and a little money – very little – and he took those. But he could not find the treasure of the Spadas.

'Years passed. The famous prayer book stayed in the family, and my friend, the Prince, now owned it. Like many people before me, I looked through all the family papers – through rooms full of papers. Where was the treasure of the Spadas? I found nothing. I read the history of the Borgia family. Cesare Borgia took all the Rospigliosis' money – true – but I found no information about the Spada treasure. I was sure that the treasure was still hidden somewhere.

'My friend died and left everything to me. He asked me to write a history of the Spada family.

'In 1807, a month before I became a prisoner, I was reading some papers. I fell asleep. It was evening when I woke up. The only light was from the fire. I felt for a piece of paper. I wanted to get a light for the lamp from the fire. I didn't want to burn any important papers, but I remembered a piece of plain white paper in the prayer book. I took it and put a corner in the fire.

'The fire began to burn the paper. Suddenly, I saw yellow writing! I quickly put out the fire, and looked at the paper. There were words on it. You could only read them when the paper was hot. I burnt a lot of the paper, but the last piece is in your hands.'

23

Dantes looked again at the yellow writing.

'And now,' said Faria, 'look at this.' He gave Dantes a second piece of paper with broken lines of writing on it. 'Put the two pieces together.'

'Yes,' Dantes said. 'I understand. But the writing on the second piece is different.'

'It is my writing,' said Faria. 'I thought about it and completed the old paper. When I understood the words, I left immediately. But the government was afraid of me. When I went on board the ship, soldiers took me prisoner.'

Faria looked at Dantes. 'And now, my dear man,' he said, 'you know as much as I do. If we ever escape together, half this treasure is yours. If I die here, all of the treasure is yours. You are my son. You were born to me in this prison. God sent you to help a sad old prisoner.'

'Thank you,' said the young man to Faria. 'But we will never have the treasure, because we won't leave this prison. My real treasure is your teaching and your wise words.'

Chapter 10   The Death of Faria

The days passed. Faria talked about his treasure, and he thought about ways of escape for his young friend.

'I am afraid that I will lose the letter,' he said to Dantes. 'Learn it – every word.' Then he burnt the paper.

Faria could not use his arm and leg, but his words and thoughts were clear. He continued to teach Dantes history and English and other subjects. He also taught him to make things – a useful skill for a prisoner. They were always busy. Dantes worked hard; he wanted to forget the past.

◆

On May 25th 1498. Cesare Borgia
invited me to dinner. He wants to kill
me. He wants all my money.
When I die give everything to Guido Spada.
It is hidden safely on the island of Monte Cristo.
Guido knows the place because we visited
it together. All my gold and money are there.
Lift up the twenty-second rock from the
beach at the east end of the island.
Find the steps that go underground.
Break into the second room. The treasure
is in the north east corner of the room.

Cesare Spada
May 25th 1498

One night, Edmond woke up suddenly. He heard a weak voice call his name through the darkness. He moved his bed, took out the stone, and hurried along the underground path. The other end of it was open. It was dark, but he saw the old, white-faced man holding on to the end of his bed in great pain.

'Ah, my dear friend,' said Faria. 'You understand, don't you? You know that the time has come.'

'Don't say that!' cried Dantes. 'I have saved you once. I will save you again.'

He quickly lifted up the foot of the bed and took out the little bottle. There was still some red liquid in it. 'Look,' he cried. 'There is still some in here. Tell me what to do.'

'There is no hope,' Faria replied. 'But you can try to save my life. Do the same thing, but don't wait too long. If I don't get better, pour the rest into my mouth. Now put me on my bed.'

Edmond took the old man in his arms and put him on the bed.

'Dear friend,' said Faria, 'you are good to me. You bring me great happiness. If you escape, go to Monte Cristo. Take the treasure and enjoy it. God go with you!'

Dantes waited, holding the bottle of liquid in his hand. When it seemed to be the right time, he poured a little of the liquid into Faria's mouth. Then he waited. He waited for ten minutes, half an hour. Then he put the bottle to Faria's mouth and poured in the rest of the liquid.

Faria moved. His eyes opened. He gave a little cry. Then silence. Edmond sat with his hand on his friend's heart. The heart became weaker and weaker. And then the old man's body slowly went cold.

Dantes went down into the underground path and put back the stones behind him. He was lucky. A few minutes later, the guard arrived. He went first to Dantes' room. Then he went on to Faria's room with his breakfast and some clothes.

'What is happening in my friend's room?' Dantes thought. 'I must know.' He went down the underground path and heard the guard's cries.

Other guards came. 'Finally,' one of them, 'the old man has gone to look for his treasure. I hope that he has a good journey!'

'And now we can prepare him for his grave,' another man said. 'Put him in a simple bag of plain cloth. That is enough for a grave at the Chateau d'If!'

Then there was silence.

'Perhaps they have gone away,' Edmond thought. 'But I am not sure, so I can't go inside.'

After an hour he heard a noise. It was the governor, and there was someone with him.

'Yes,' said an unknown voice, 'Faria is dead.'

'I am sure that he is,' the governor said. 'But by the rules of the prison, we must check.'

Dantes heard more footsteps. People went in and out of the room. Then he heard someone pull a large piece of cloth along the floor. There was another sound from the bed when somebody put a heavy weight on it.

'In the evening,' said the governor. 'At about ten or eleven.'

'Shall we stay with the body?'

'No. That isn't necessary. Lock the door.'

The steps went away and the voices disappeared. Someone locked the door. Then there was silence, the deepest of all silences – the silence of death.

Dantes lifted the stone. He looked carefully round the room. There was nobody there. He went in.

Chapter 11   The Grave of the Chateau d'If

On the bed Dantes saw a long bag of dirty cloth. The body of his friend Faria lay inside it. 'Alone! I am alone again,' Dantes thought. And then he stopped. He looked at the bag and a strange thought came to him. 'Only dead people leave this prison. I can take the place of the dead!'

There was no time to think about it. Dantes opened the bag with Faria's knife. He took the body from the bag and carried it along the underground path to his own room. He laid the body on his bed and pulled the bedclothes over its head. Then he kissed the cold face and turned it to the wall.

'The guard will think that I am asleep,' Dantes said to himself.

He returned to Faria's room, took off his clothes and hid them. Then he got inside the bag, and lay exactly like the dead body. 'I have made my plan,' he thought. 'Will the men discover me when they carry the bag outside? Will they find a living man, not a dead body? If that happens, I will cut open the bag from top to bottom with the knife. Then I will escape. If they try to catch me, I will use the knife.

'Perhaps they will put me in the grave, and cover me with earth. It will be night. I only hope that the grave is not too deep.'

Another thought came to him. 'When the guard brings my evening meal at seven o'clock, will he notice Faria's body in my bed? But no, I am often in bed when the man comes. He just puts the food on the table and goes away again in silence. If he speaks to me this time, what will happen then? When he gets no answer, will he go to the bed?'

Dantes waited for the cries of the guard. But the hours passed, and the prison was quiet. Finally, Edmond heard footsteps outside. He must be brave now, braver than ever before. The footsteps stopped outside the door.

'There are two of them,' Dantes decided. He heard them

Dantes opened the bag with Faria's knife.

put down some wood. 'They are going to carry the body on that,' he thought.

The door opened. Through the cloth of the bag, he saw two shadows come to the ends of his bed. Another man stood at the door with the lamp.

'He was a thin old man, but he is heavy.' One man was lifting up his head. The other man lifted his feet.

'Have you tied it on?' the first speaker asked.

'Not yet – we don't want to carry unnecessary weight!' the other man replied. 'I can do that when we get there.'

'"Tied it on." Tied *what* on?' thought Dantes.

The men put the body on the piece of wood. Then they moved up the steps.

Suddenly, Dantes felt the cold, fresh night air. The men walked about twenty metres, then stopped and put the body down. One of them went away. Dantes heard the sound of his shoes on the stone. 'Where am I?' he asked himself.

'Here it is. I have found it.'

Edmond heard the man put a heavy weight on to the ground next to him. Then he tied the weight round Dantes' feet.

'Is that tied carefully?' asked the other man.

'Yes. It won't come off,' was the answer.

The men lifted Dantes up again, and they began to walk. Now Dantes heard the sound of waves against the rocks.

'We are finally here,' said one of the men.

'Don't stop yet,' said the other man. 'You know very well that the last one fell on the rocks. Don't you remember that the governor was angry with us?'

They went five or six more steps, then they lifted Dantes by his head and by his feet.

'One!' said the men. 'Two! Three – and away!'

They threw Dantes into the air. He was falling, falling. A heavy weight pulled him quickly down. Finally, with a great noise, he fell into the cold water. When he hit the water, he gave a cry. Then the water closed over him.

'They have thrown me into the sea!' Dantes cried to himself. 'They tied a big stone to my feet. It is pulling me down to the bottom of the sea. This is the grave of the Chateau d'If – the sea!'

Chapter 12   The *Young Amelia*

Dantes was wise. He kept his mouth shut after that first cry of surprise. In his right hand he still held the knife. He quickly cut open the bag, got one arm out and then his body. The stone pulled him down and down, and he felt very weak. But he reached down and cut the stone free. Then he swam quickly to the top of the water, and the stone fell to the bottom of the sea.

Dantes felt the night air on his face. He began to swim under the water because he did not want the guards to see him.

When he came up again, he was nearly a hundred metres from the prison. Above him, he saw a black and stormy sky. In front of him lay the great black sea. Behind him, blacker than the sea, blacker than the clouds, stood the Chateau d'If. It was a large and terrible place. The rocks around it seemed to reach out to take him back. And on the highest rock there were two men holding a lamp.

'They are looking at the sea,' Dantes thought. 'Perhaps they heard me shout.' He went down again under the water and stayed there for a long time.

When he came up again, he could not see the light. He began to swim out to sea. He swam for hours; he was trying to reach an island.

'In two or three hours,' he thought, 'the guard will go into my room. He will find the body of my poor friend. He will look for me and not find me, and then he will call for help. The soldiers will discover the underground path. They will question the men who threw me into the sea. They will send boats of soldiers to find the escaped prisoner. Everyone will search for a hungry man without clothes. Soldiers will look for me in Marseilles, and the governor and his men will search for me on the sea. I am cold. I am hungry. I have lost my knife. Oh, my God! Help me – oh, help me!'

After Dantes said this prayer, he looked towards the Chateau d'If. He saw a small ship, coming out from Marseilles. It was moving quickly out to sea.

It came near him. He shouted and waved his hand. The ship turned towards him, and let down a boat.

There were two men in the boat. Dantes began to swim to it, but he was too weak. He gave a cry, and one of the men in the boat shouted, 'Be strong! We are coming!'

Dantes heard their words. A wave passed over him. He came up to the top of the water, and then he went down again. The water closed over his head. 'I am dying!' he thought. Then someone caught him by the hair and pulled him up. After that, he heard and saw nothing.

When Dantes opened his eyes, he was on board the ship. 'Where are we going?' he thought. He looked out through a small window. 'We are leaving the Chateau d'If behind!'

The captain came to see him.

'I am a seaman, and I lost my ship in the storm,' Dantes told him.

'You can stay on my ship,' the captain said. 'But you will have to work.' Suddenly, a loud noise rang across the waters. 'Hey! What is that?' cried the captain.

'A prisoner has escaped from the Chateau d'If,' replied Dantes.

Dantes began to swim to it, but he was too weak.

'Is *he* the escaped prisoner?' the captain thought. He looked at Dantes. 'Does it matter? Even if it is him, he will be useful to us.'

The ship was called the *Young Amelia*. It carried goods to quiet shores on dark nights. There were no customs officers in these places, so the captain did not pay money to the government for the goods.

At first the captain did not tell Dantes about his business. 'I do not know this man,' he thought. 'Perhaps he is a government officer.' But after some days, he started to like Dantes.

◆

The ship reached Livorno. Edmond asked a man there to shave him and cut his hair. When the job was finished, he asked for a mirror. He saw the changes in his face.

'When I went to the Chateau d'If, my face was round and open. It was the face of a young and happy man,' he said to himself. Now his face was longer. His mouth was harder and stronger. His eyes were deep and thoughtful, and his skin was whiter. Even his voice was softer and sadder.

'I don't know myself,' he thought. 'I am a stranger.'

Next, he went to buy some clothes. Then, a changed man, he went back on board the *Young Amelia*.

The men of the *Young Amelia* worked hard for their captain. They spent very little time in Livorno. The captain wanted to get the goods out of the city quickly, and to take them to Corsica.

They sailed away. Edmond was happy on the open sea. 'I often dreamed about this in prison,' he thought.

Early next morning, the captain found Dantes. The two men stood at the side of the ship, and looked at some great rocks. The sun shone in the sky and coloured the rocks a soft pink. It was the island of Monte Cristo.

'I can jump over the side of the ship,' Dantes thought, 'and

He looked again at the island.

swim to the island in an hour. But if I do that, how will I get the treasure away? I must wait. I waited for years to be free. I can wait for a few months to be rich.' He looked again at the island. 'Perhaps the treasure is only a dream, a dream of Faria's. But there was Prince Spada's letter. That seemed real.' Dantes repeated the letter to himself from the beginning to the end; he remembered every word.

Night came, and Edmond watched the island. It was beautiful with the colours of the evening, then slowly it hid itself in the darkness.

'How can I reach Monte Cristo and bring the treasure back safely? The treasure is mine. But I have no money for a small boat to get it.'

He thought about this problem all the time.

◆

They returned from Corsica to Livorno. One evening, in Livorno, the captain asked Dantes to come to an important meeting. Edmond went with the captain to see other ships' captains. They talked about a ship from Turkey which was carrying expensive cloth. They wanted to find a quiet place and meet this ship, buy the cloth and then take it to the coast of France.

'We need a quiet place where there are no customs officers,' one man said. 'A place where nobody will see us.'

'The best place is the island of Monte Cristo,' said the captain of the *Young Amelia*. 'Nobody lives on the island, and no customs officers ever go there.'

They decided to sail to Monte Cristo the next night.

Chapter 13   Monte Cristo

And so, by a lucky accident, Dantes reached the island of Monte Cristo. The *Young Amelia* was first at the meeting place. Dantes was the first person to reach the shore.

The men knew the island well. Dantes questioned Jacopo, the man who saved him from the sea. 'Where shall we spend the night?'

'On the ship, of course.'

'I must find the place where Spada hid the treasure,' Dantes thought. 'There is an opening somewhere – but where? Perhaps Spada hid it with stones, or perhaps it is now covered with trees and plants. But I must wait for the morning.'

Just then a boat arrived and came close to the shore. The business began. As he worked, Dantes worried. 'Did I say too much to Jacopo? Will the men learn about the treasure?' No. His secret was still safe.

Next morning, the men rested. When Dantes quietly walked away, nobody seemed surprised. He climbed high, until the men on the shore looked very small. Then he found a path that was cut by a stream between two walls of rock. He followed it. 'The treasure is near here,' he thought.

As he went along the coast, he looked at everything carefully. 'These stones have marks on them. A man made these marks!' He came to the twenty-first stone, and the marks stopped. But there was no opening, just one large rock. 'This rock is so big. I don't think anybody can move it! It is too heavy. I must start again.' And he turned and went back to his friends.

The men on the shore were cooking a meal. They were sitting down to eat when they saw Dantes. He was jumping from rock to rock towards them. All eyes turned to him. But then they saw him fall! They all ran to him, but Jacopo reached him first.

Edmond was not moving. 'Is he dead?' Jacopo thought.

After some time Dantes opened his eyes. 'My knee hurts very badly,' he said, 'and my head and my legs feel heavy.'

They wanted to carry him to the shore. But when they touched him, he gave a cry of pain. 'Don't move me!' he cried. 'The pain is too great.'

He did not want any food, but he told the other men to have their meal. 'I only need to rest,' he said. 'When you return, I will feel better.' The sailors went away.

They returned an hour later. 'He is not getting better,' one of the sailors said. 'His pain seems to be worse.'

'I must sail this morning,' the captain said to Dantes. 'Won't you try to get up?'

Dantes tried to stand up, but each time he fell back. With each fall he cried out with pain.

'He has broken his leg,' the captain said in a low voice. 'But he is a very good man, and we can't leave him. We will try to carry him on board the ship.'

'No,' Dantes said. 'The pain is too bad. Don't move me. Leave me here.'

'No,' said the captain, 'we won't leave until evening. I don't want people to think that we left a good man like you on this empty island.'

But Dantes told him to go. 'No, no,' he said to the captain. 'I was stupid, and I must suffer for my mistake. Leave me a small amount of food and an axe. I will build myself a hut.'

The captain turned towards his ship. It was waiting just off the shore, ready for sea. 'What shall we do?' he asked. 'We can't leave you here; but we can't stay.'

'Go. Please go,' cried Dantes.

'We will be away for more than a week,' the captain said. 'Then we will make a special journey to get you.'

Dantes spoke again. 'If, in two or three days, you see a fishing boat, ask them to come here for me. I will pay them to take me to Livorno. If you don't meet a fishing boat, please come back for me.'

'Listen, Captain,' said Jacopo. 'I will stay with him.'

'You will say goodbye to your part of the money from this business to stay with me?'

'Yes,' said Jacopo immediately.

A strange look passed over Dantes' face. He pressed Jacopo's hand. 'You are a good, kind-hearted friend,' he said to Jacopo. 'God will love you for your kindness. But I don't want anyone to stay with me. I will be all right.'

The men left the things that Edmond wanted. Then they went back to the ship. Two or three times they turned round and waved to him, and Edmond waved back.

'They are rough, dangerous men,' Dantes said to himself, 'but they are good friends.'

He pulled himself up carefully to the top of the rock. He watched the ship leave. Like a beautiful white bird, it sailed out over the sea.

Chapter 14   Treasure

Edmond climbed carefully down from the rocks.

'I didn't really fall. I wanted the men to leave me here. I don't want to fall and hurt myself now!' he thought.

He followed the line of marks on the stones again. They started from a small place on the shore. Only a small ship could land there. 'But Spada's boat landed here,' Dantes said to himself. The marks ended at the large round rock.

'But,' thought Edmond, 'how did Prince Spada lift this heavy rock into this place? Twenty men couldn't move a rock like this.' Suddenly a thought came to him. 'They didn't lift this rock into its place – it fell here!'

He jumped from the rock to look at the ground above it.

'Somebody cut a path here, and moved the rock down it. They put a large stone here to hold it in its place. Now the stone is almost hidden by the grass. But the rock does not fit perfectly. The holes are full of small stones and earth.'

Dantes cut away these small stones at the top, and after ten minutes he put his arm into the hole. He took his axe and cut wood from a strong tree. Then he put one end of the wood into the hole and pulled on the other. The rock moved. Again he pulled. The rock moved from its place, and then fell back again. Dantes rested. He gave a last, strong pull. The rock fell down the hill into the sea.

In the place of the rock, Dantes saw a large square stone, with a ring in the centre of it. He felt weak, so he waited for a minute. Then he put the wood into the ring and lifted the stone. He saw steps going down into the darkness of an underground room.

But there was some light down there, and the air was fresh. Both the light and air came in through small holes in the rock above his head. Dantes looked into the corners of the underground room. There was nothing in them.

He remembered the words of the letter: 'Break into the second room.' He was in the first room, and he must now find the second room. He began to hit the wall with his axe. In one place the sound of the axe was a little different. He hit it again. The hard rock broke away easily. Behind it there was a wall of square white stones.

'Somebody built this opening. Then they painted it to look like rock,' Dantes thought.

He felt very weak. He put the axe on the ground and went up the steps, out into the open air.

'I have not eaten any food for hours. I am not hungry, but I must eat.' He ate a little bread and took a drink from his water bottle. Then he returned. He was able to use the axe more easily now.

'This wall in front of me is only made of stones, one on top of another.' He pulled them off, one by one. Finally, Dantes broke the wall into the second room. It was smaller and darker than the first one. He waited for fresh air to fill the room. Then he went in.

There was a dark corner to the left of the opening. He looked round this second room. 'If there is treasure,' he thought, 'it is hidden in that dark corner.'

Dantes went to the corner and began to move the earth. Suddenly, his axe hit a hard place. He lifted the axe to hit the place again. Again he heard the same sound.

'It is a great wooden chest. There are strong pieces of metal round it,' he thought, finally. He went outside.

There, he stood and thought. Then he took a dry piece of wood, lit it, and went down again. He looked at the top of the chest. It was about a metre long and half a metre wide. In the centre, there was a piece of silver in the wood. There was a mark on the silver – the mark of the Spada family.

'The treasure is here!' Dantes thought. He tried to lift the box but he couldn't. He tried to open it, but there was no key. He took his axe to break it open. The top came away; the wood was old and soft.

There were three smaller boxes inside. In the first box there were gold coins from many different countries. In the second box were bars of gold. From the third box, Edmond took a handful of gold rings.

He touched, felt and looked at the treasure. Then Edmond ran quickly back to the steps. He jumped up on a rock and looked out at the sea. He was alone – alone with this great treasure! Was he awake – or was it a dream?

He touched, felt and looked at the treasure.

Chapter 15   At Marseilles

The next morning Dantes climbed to the top of the highest rock. He looked for houses and men on the island, but there were none. It really was an empty place.

He returned to the treasure place and went into the second room. He took gold and some coins and hid them safely in his clothing. Then he covered the chest with earth, and put sand over the place.

'Nobody can see anything now,' he thought. He put a large stone over the opening and covered it with earth. He placed some quick-growing plants in the earth. He went over the ground all round the place, and hid every mark. 'Nobody will find this place.'

He waited for his friends to return. That was not easy. He did not want to sit and guard his great treasure. He wanted to return and live with men.

'These riches will give me great power. Danglars, Caderousse, even Villefort cannot hurt me now. I don't need to worry about them. With all this money, I can bring happiness to the people who are nearest to my heart!'

◆

After six days, the *Young Amelia* returned. Dantes went down to the shore. He walked slowly. 'My leg still hurts,' he said. 'Did your business go well?'

'We got the goods safely to land,' the captain said. 'But when we finished, a government ship from Toulon came after us. We needed you – you are a good sailor and we needed your help. Luckily night came, and we escaped. We have brought the *Young Amelia* to Monte Cristo to get you.'

Dantes went on board, and the ship sailed for Livorno.

In Livorno, Dantes sold four of the smallest rings to a

shopkeeper. Edmond was afraid. 'Will he ask where I found these rings? I am only a poor seaman.' But the shopkeeper said nothing.

The next day, Dantes went to the captain. 'My uncle has died and left me a large amount of money,' he said. 'I want to leave the ship.'

'I am sad to lose you,' the captain said. 'Can't you stay?'

'No,' Dantes said. 'I must leave the *Young Amelia*.'

He gave fine presents to all the men. He gave a new ship and some money to his best friend, Jacopo. After that, he left Livorno and went to Genoa.

In Genoa he saw a boat builder. The man had a beautiful little ship on the water. 'I built this boat for an Englishman,' the boat builder said.

It was very small. 'I can sail it myself, alone, without help' Dantes thought. 'And it is very fast. No other ship on the water will catch it.'

Dantes offered a lot of money for the boat and asked the builder for the ship's papers.

'The Englishman will not return for some time,' the boat builder said. 'I am sure that I can build another boat for him.' So he agreed to sell the boat.

He offered to find seamen for the ship, but Dantes said, 'I don't need anyone. But make me a hidden place on the ship, near the top of my bed.'

The builder promised to do the work the next day.

◆

Dantes sailed away from Genoa alone, and arrived at Monte Cristo on the second day.

He took his boat to a different place on the shore. There was nobody on the island, and the treasure was still there.

Early the next day, he began to carry his treasure on board. By evening it was safely hidden in the secret place.

One fine morning, a small but beautiful boat sailed into Marseilles. Dantes tied it up near some steps. 'I left Marseilles just here, many years ago, to go to the Chateau d'If,' he thought.

The customs officers came on board to look at the ship's papers. A soldier stood near the steps. Even now, Dantes was afraid when he saw a soldier.

Edmond now had a different name – a rich man's name. He showed the officers the ship's papers.

'This boat is owned by the Count of Monte Cristo,' the papers said.

The customs officers wanted to please the rich ship owner. 'The count can go on shore now, if he wants to,' they said. 'There is no problem with his papers.'

Old Nicolas, a seaman from the *Pharaoh,* was one of the first men that he met on shore. Dantes went straight to Nicolas and asked him a number of questions. He watched the man's face carefully, but Nicolas did not know him. Dantes gave him some money and turned away. Soon he heard a shout.

'Stop!' Nicolas called. Dantes turned back. 'This coin is gold, not silver!' said the good man. 'It is too much.'

'Yes, my good man,' said Dantes, 'I made a small mistake. Thank you for telling me. Here, take this second gold coin.'

Nicolas was surprised. He could not speak.

Dantes continued on his way. Every tree, every street brought back memories of the past. He walked until he saw his father's house.

The door was shut, but from inside he heard the sound of quietly moving feet. Then there was a silence that was broken by a weak cry of pain.

Someone said very softly, 'Yes, soon. Very soon now. But you must be strong.'

Every tree, every street brought back memories of the past. He walked until he saw his father's house.

Dantes put out his hand to open the door. But his hand fell back to his side. He could not move.

'But I tell you – he is here,' said the weak voice again. 'Go and call him in?'

'Try to get a little sleep now. Perhaps when you wake –'

'I tell you – he is here. I saw him come up the street. I saw him stand and look up at this window with his dear eyes. He has changed. Tell him to come quickly. Tell him that Death is waiting at my side.' The voice grew stronger. 'Open the door, I say, and bring him in!'

There were footsteps. The door opened slowly – and Mercedes stood there.

She saw him. At first, she did not know him. Then she fell forward with a cry.

'It is you!' she cried. Then, taking his hand, she pulled him into the room. 'Come quickly. He wants to see you.'

The old eyes looked up at him, dark and beautiful with a last silent look of love. Then the eyes closed.

'Kiss me,' he said. 'Hold me in your arms, Edmond. Death, you can come and take me now!'

◆

Napoleon returned to France in 1815. Danglars left the country, and nobody saw him again.

'Caderousse is still alive,' said Mercedes, 'but he is very poor.'

◆

'Look,' said old Nicolas to a soldier standing by the steps. Far away on the Mediterranean Sea, there was a white sail.

'He has gone,' said old Nicolas, 'that rich Count.'

'Yes. I saw him go,' replied the soldier. 'And her.'

ACTIVITIES

Chapters 1–5

Before you read

1 Read the Introduction to the book. The story is about France in the 1800s. Which of these people and places were real?

Edmond Dantes   Napoleon   Marseilles   Mr Morrel   Chateau d'If   Cesare Borgia

2 Find these words in your dictionary. Use them in the sentences below.

board   captain   courtyard   God   ruler

   a The .... is the most important officer on the ship.

   b A .... is the head of a country's government.

   c There was a .... at the back of the house.

   d The man climbed on .... the ship.

   e Do you believe in ....?

3 Find the words in *italics* in your dictionary. Are the sentences true?

   a *Goods* are things that are bought and sold.

   b A *governor* does the job of a policeman.

   c People used *lamps* to light a dark room.

   d An important person has *power* over other people.

   e The *shore* is the place where the land meets the sea.

   f *Treasure* is a name for an underground place.

After you read

4 Why does Dantes stop at Elba? What happens on the island?

5 What feelings are there between these people? Give reasons for your answers.

   a Edmond and Mercedes

   b Danglars and Edmond

   c Mr Morrel and Edmond

Chapters 6-10

Before you read

6 Why is Edmond in the Chateau d'If? What do you think will happen to him there?

7 Find the words in *italics* in your dictionary. Answer the questions.

    a Do *bars* on a window help you get out or keep you in?

    b Is water a *liquid* or a gas?

    c Is a *prayer* a message to God or to a friend?

    d Is a *grave* a place for a living person or a dead one?

After you read

8 Why is the prayer book important to the story? What does Faria find inside it?

9 Work with another student. Act out the conversation when Faria tells Dantes about the treasure.

Chapters 11–15

Before you read

10 'The treasure is here!' Who do you think says these words? What is 'the treasure'?

11 Find these words in your dictionary. What do they mean?

    customs chest mark axe coins

    a a sharp tool for cutting down trees

    b money for the government on goods that are brought into the country

    c gold or silver money

    d a letter, number or sign that is cut into wood or stone.

    e a large box

After you read

12 When Dantes sees himself in a mirror, he says 'I am a stranger.' Describe the changes in him.

13 Why does Dantes return to Marseilles? What does he do there?

Writing

14 You are Dantes and you are a prisoner in the Chateau d'If. Imagine that you can write a letter to your father. Describe your life, and your new friend Faria.

15 Write a newspaper report about Dantes' escape from the Chateau d'If.

16 Write about these people. What is good and what is bad about them?

Villefort   the captain of the *Young Amelia*

17 Imagine that it is a year later. What are Dantes and Mercedes doing now? Write about it.

Answers for the Activities in this book are published in our free resource packs for teachers, the Penguin Readers Factsheets, or available on a separate sheet. Please write to your local Pearson Education office or to: Marketing Department, Penguin Longman Publishing, 5 Bentinck Street, London W1M 5RN.